THEY LIFT THEIR
WINGS TO CRY

THEY LIFT THEIR WINGS TO CRY

Poems

Brooks Haxton

Alfred A. Knopf   New York   2008

THIS IS A BORZOI BOOK
PUBLISHED BY ALFRED A. KNOPF

Copyright © 2008 by Brooks Haxton
All rights reserved. Published in the United States by
Alfred A. Knopf, a division of Random House, Inc.,
New York, and in Canada by Random House of
Canada, Limited, Toronto.
www.aaknopf.com

Grateful acknowledgment is made to S. Fischer Verlag GmbH for permission to
translate "Es war Erde in Ihnen" from *Die Niemandsrose* by Paul Celan, copyright ©
1963 by S. Fischer Verlag GmbH, Frankfurt am Main, Germany, translated here by
Brooks Haxton. Translated by permission of S. Fischer Verlag GmbH.

Library of Congress Cataloging-in-Publication Data
Haxton, Brooks, [date]
They lift their wings to cry : poems / by Brooks Haxton.—1st ed.
p. cm.
ISBN 978-0-307-26845-7
I. Title.
PS3558.A825T47 2008
811'.54—dc22   2008005766

Manufactured in the United States of America
First Edition

for my mother,

Josephine Ayres Haxton,

love always

And thank you for the pile of driftwood.
Am I needed at the sea?

—KENNETH KOCH

Contents

THEY LIFT THEIR WINGS TO CRY

LOOKING UP PAST MIDNIGHT INTO THE SPIN OF THE CATALPA BLOSSOMS

I came home drunk without my key
and lay down in the yard to think.
Inside my skull on damp grass thoughts
spun inward. Whorls of a magnetic field
exfoliated under the solar wind,
so that the northern lights above me
trembled. No: that was the porch light
blurred by tears. Moths slammed
headfirst into the lightbulb. Maybe
they needed bigger brains. Me, too.
I closed my blurry eyes, and springs
flowed underwater in my sleep.

WHEN I CAME AWAKE

From the floor of the well I saw
leaves larger than my hands
and purple fruit, a brown finch
opened his beak to sing,
and golden trumpets hung
from vines at the lip, pouring
the warm smell of magnolia
from my childhood down the wall.
The stone floor made sleep difficult.
But when I put my ear to it
I heard waves far off breaking
into the face of a cliff.

BERT, IN MEMORY, AND HERB ROBERT

to Roberta Miller

In a dream
at dawn you came,
your face
in old age

animate, although
I could not hear
what words your lips
were making,

and then, waking,
I went out,
the way we used to do,
to find wildflowers.

Under the bloom-spent
pussy willow and magnolia,
the forget-me-nots
were blooming, sky-blue

tiny flowers yellow
at the eye, a white star
where the ridges are
between the petals.

Nearby grew
herb Robert, called
by your name, smaller,
streaked with redder veins

than wild geranium, its cousin
we saw earlier, which now,
Bert, like your voice, is gone.
And in a few days

early buttercup,
ground ivy, bleeding heart,
all will have been
and will not be,

as now the trillium,
violet, and lily
of a month ago
have gone away.

I set these names,
in any case,
the gone and going,
all together, all at once,

for you, who came to me
among the speedwell
which we call
veronica, the very icon

of God's loving face,
whose pain that flower's

namesake soothed
when he was soon to die.

For you,
whom flowers
and their names
gave pleasure,

Bert, I set these
on the page to fade,
that your gone voice and mine
may join in praise.

THE CRY OF THE SNOWY TREE CRICKET

. . . instead of sleep,
instead of her touch, comes your chirp
—Meleagros, 1st century BCE

The number of chirps in 13 seconds plus 40 gives
a good estimate of the temperature in degrees
Fahrenheit.
—Borror and White, *A Field Guide to Insects,* 1970

Separate at first, like tiny hinges on the twilight,
   crickets finding each the others' rhythm
      sing in unison all night.

   The bigger ones that dance in courtship,
brown-black maestros of the triple chirp, my children
   turn up under the fallen leaves by noon,
while these—the pale green, small, nocturnal ones
     with broad, transparent wings—
      we almost never see.

We hear them, washboard ridge on one wing strummed
    by the hardened edge of the other.
     Both wings, lifted, vibrate,
amplifying the chirp that Frenchmen call their cry:
   ils crient: they cry. But what they mean,
what cellos for that matter mean, we cannot say,
      or how it sounds to them,
   with auditory membranes on their forelimbs
more acute at higher frequencies than human ears.

   Shut, solo, in the attic from predawn till noon,
I mutter scraps of phrases to myself, and claim
   to know, as crickets cannot know, that I exist.

Their eggs, all winter frozen in the bark,
　　by summer hatch out of a paste of dung,
　the white nymphs tinier than flakes of snow,
which do not melt, but grow, and molt, and grow,
　and finally chirp, more slowly by exact degrees,
until the cold brings back the frost and silence.

　　Under the window, meanwhile, drifting
at the verge of sleep, just conscious of immersion
　　in their song, though not quite sure where
　　consciousness resides, or what it is,
　　　　I listen. Males in thousands
　　intimate what females of their species,
　　　lacking auditory organs, cannot hear.

And yet the lifting of a cricket's wings to cry
　　　　exposes on the upper torso
　　scent glands that secrete a liquor
　which the female cricket thinks superb.
　　　She finds the male by scent
　　and climbs (oblivious to any song,
　the night dimensional for her with musk)
　　onto his back, to lap that dewdrop
of incarnate being. Then, her ministrations
　　hushing him, they mate. This poem also
　cries, and hushes as your mind draws near.

DATURA

When the full moon rises
and the sphinx moth, hidden
all day, hovers into the twilight
between smoky blurs of wings,
in midair she spools loose
her tongue, and dips her body
into the grail cup of the fumes
for which to be the sphinx
at nightfall is to yearn.

ISAAC'S ROOM, EMPTY, 4 A.M.

From the dark tree at his window
blossoms battered by the rain
fell into the summer grass, white
horns, all spattered down the throat
with purple ink, while unseen birds,
with creaks and peeps
and whistles, started
the machinery of daybreak.

MY FATHER'S SUIT

The suit we chose was navy blue.
He sold them, hundreds,
which we helped to fit,
our hands impersonal,
adept, that signed the papers now,
while someone dressed his body
in the suit. Without cosmetics,
in the viewing room, the face
looked green and uninhabited,
lips wide and thickly set,
no ghost of him, not sad,
not funny, not one bit
afraid—the freckle on the hand,
hair, veins, what had been his,
without him now, extraneous, inane,
brow under my trembling right palm
cool with an inhuman density,
as though immovable, but not.

FACE TO FACE

Sunlight under your eyebrow knits
the iris into a bronzen veil.
The eyelids droop. Your face and mine,
unseeing, kiss, and this entails
beyond the soul the fingertip
along the inner arm and where
the earlobe joins the jaw.
Without your quiddity
of anklebone and laugh,
the godhead is a botched
hypothesis of love. Forgive
my saying so. A moment's
yearning puts to shame all thought
of love sufficient to itself.

BAREFOOT

Just as the big toe and the ball
of my right foot pressed
their imprint into the mud,
pushing off and rising,
my left heel sank back
into the mold of the earth.

HER HIGH SCHOOL FLAME
RETIRES AT 65 AND MOVES BACK
INTO HIS CHILDHOOD HOME

Beyond the tilting front deck
with its rotted columns, inside,
where the sun through warped
sidelights of leaded glass fell
onto an oak floor spotted
with the heads of ancient nails,
she paused at the foot of his staircase,
left hand stroking the curve
of the maple handrail, followed him
through the built-in ashwood pantry
layered now with seven coats of paint,
and crossed the worn linoleum
through the kitchen, out, into his bower
of weeds and weed trees. There,
for the first time since they kissed
good-bye forever, they could talk.

LETTER FROM SYRACUSE

to George Tatge

The year we met, I read out loud old songs.
In one Colin Muset sang after the Crusades
about the urge to stay home in the winter.
Why go out on horseback, torching
villages, to get his bounty as a thief,
when he could roast a capon at his fireplace?

At my fireplace, you played your guitar
and sang me sambas in the Portuguese, and now
your children, older than we were back then,
speak Florentine, and mine speak Yankee. So do I,
not well.

       The first day snowless in a month,
with snow piles in the parking lot
three times my height, your letter comes.
Between the lines I hear guitar, your voice
as cheerful in its tenor as Colin, whose blessing,
if I thought I'd hit the notes, I'd sing you:
clear wine in a warm house.

          Lately, I've been reading
poems of exile. Su Tung-P'o, after his early fame
at court, in middle age climbed into the mountains
of his banishment, and built himself a house
he called Snow Hall, where frozen ink sometimes

would stop his writing. Called back, found
treasonous again, and sent away, he grew old
speaking tenderly about new neighbors on Hainan,
the farthest island in the empire.

                    Ovid, our age,
got sent packing to the eastern edge of nowhere,
and he whined nonstop for years. He said
the bay at Tomis froze shut for the winter.
Please! It's true he'd lost a wife, his third,
and what's worse, Rome, a city full
of devotees and lovers. He felt cold,
I'll grant you, but the Baltic at Gdansk
does not freeze shut, much less the Black at Tomis.

Larry, on the other hand, a local guy
who put the walls and insulation in the attic
for my study, knows bad weather. Years ago,
he says, his girlfriend had a camp that caught
the weather off the lake. One afternoon
they wake up, raise the shade, and see
a snowdrift covering the window. Door,
same thing: they open it: a wall, full frame:
it's soft, but smooth like marble in a mausoleum.
Upstairs, they look down: no car, just drifts, none
vaguely car-shaped. Larry shimmies out the window
up there, pokes around between his snowshoes
with a broomstick, finally hits the car roof,
down four feet: thunk. Now what?

                    Here,
we drive each other crazy, same as in the summer,

but it's looking up, no snow so far
today. Clear wine. The house is warm, cars
visible. There is a monster tooth
of ice latched into the valley in the eaves,
which hangs two stories almost to the ground
and weighs more than a wrecking ball. The roof
I mention only in my prayers.

But Andy,
my good friend, a fellow Southerner, says,
back when he was teaching in Duluth and lived
on Lake Superior, storms pushed ice slabs
up the bank like ramps. We see that here
some winters. Next storm, breakers scoot big
chunks of ice toward shore across the ice sheet,
fast. They hit those ramps, they fly. One flew,
he tells me, into a second-story bedroom
through the wall.

My point about the weather—
and there's inside weather too: synaptic
mood fronts, humors, potent stuff, no joke,
the whole show's deadly—but my point is,
when your letter came, no snow all day.

THE INVENTION OF A WRITTEN
WORD FOR GOD IN SUMER

The wedge sank five times into the clay,
and a word, that had been spoken in a breath,
lay still until the gods' names were forgotten.
Then, when strangers took the tile in hand,
while stars sailed into the dark
beyond the world, the dead tongue
in the clay began to speak.

BEDROOM WINDOW CRUSTED THICK WITH ICE

Where molecules of water took
dictation from the cold
between the stars, crystals
in the lower margin looked
like characters in Arabic,
cuneiform, and Mandarin, six-point,
a smattering of chaos somebody
with better eyes might read.
However bundled we went out, we felt
the cold when we had entered it
begin to enter us. Misunderstanding
circumstantiates the world.

YOUR CALL FROM ECUADOR

Arcturus, you said, looked
as nonchalant down there
as it did here over the lake.
Your voice kept fading
into the breakers at your feet.
My neighbor's pickup
drove out on the ice, parked,
and three guys stumbling
in the moonlight revved their saw.
How many years ago did you
and I walk out onto that pier
in Georgia while fork lightning
sizzled in the storm surge?
We were young, sharks cruising
underfoot, and we kept laughing.
Clouds sailed overhead
at different speeds, all fast.
Then—mountain ranges, gulfs
and chasms, continents between us
all of a sudden—we were old men:
we looked up, and laughed.

KNOWLEDGE

My *Unabridged* gives "know"
twelve meanings. I would list them
if I weren't so sleepy. Are you sleepy?

You and I could sleep together
if you like. We might as well.
From reading poems in languages

nobody speaks, I recognize
cognoscere, gignoskein, and *gecnawan*
as old cognates of our verb to know.

Does knowing this make you feel sleepy
too? When I was small, I dreaded
ignorance. I feel small now,

although my hands and feet,
as you can see, grew larger
than the average size. If you feel

sleepy, yawn. Did you know *theos*
as a name for god may not imply
a person, necessarily? Your person,

on the other hand, implies to me
that holiness of being
I could no more willingly forgo

than I could forgo sleep.
To sleep with and to know
mean one thing sometimes,

although knowledge seems the opposite
of sleep. Shall I switch off
the light so we can see?

MY BRAIN STILL WORKED, I SAID

My body must have walked me home by rote,
the way a horse does with slack reins.
Brow leaking fresh blood down my face,
past midnight, I came in, and from the mirror
over the bathroom sink I called out to my wife:
I needed her. I told her I did something . . .
what, I couldn't say. She looked me in the face,
and I looked down, and gouts of blood dropped
from my forehead into the pocket of my shirt.
"What happened?" I kept asking her, but what
she told me faded into what came next.
When doctors in the ER asked what time
of year it was, my guess was wrong. The president
whose name I could remember lost eight terms before.
My brain still worked, I said: I knew poems
I had learned by heart when I was young.
I tried to make them see by quoting one:
"Time present and time past are both perhaps
present in time future, and time future
contained in time past." "Good," the doctor said.
But CAT scans on the light box worried me.
I looked down into my bandaged hands, ashamed:
I must have hurt myself. I asked my wife, "What
happened?" And the night nurse rolled her eyes.

WORM MOON

Purim, 2006

Under the veil of the penumbra,
though the blot of inner shadow
never touched it,
it shone full
into the blue cups of the crocuses
and onto the frost-scarred dirt.
This was a moon to drink,
to dance by, moon
my friend the klezmer,
who reads trope
and studies midrash, watched
by telescope with atheistic calm.

PROBLEM

*Holland (1986) and Bass (1987) regard the skull
after the pelvis as the best section of the skeleton
for reliable gender differentiation.*
—Dr. Matthias Graw, report to the FBI, 2001

My wife out of nowhere struck me
in the back of the head with a ladle.

What was that for?

                Your inion.

What?

        The ridge on your occiput.

Right. I was asking, what's
the problem.

        You, she said,
right there, and struck the spot.

GREEN LAKES STATE PARK

Falls more massive than Niagara
dug this plunge pool
thirty fathoms into the rock,
and then the glaciers and the falls
were gone. An old man
read the guidebook out loud,
while his grandson watched
a red-tailed hawk preen
in the dead top of a maple
across the lake. Big hemlocks,
white pines, cedars all around,
the little lake was calm
and very deep, clear
as old glass in the sunlight.
Meromictic, the old man read,
means partly mixed.
The laketop in November,
dense with cold, sinks
into the shadows fifty feet,
coming to rest, fresh water
on a lower depth of brine.
Blooming in the twilight underneath
is a green-and-purple layer,
one yard thick, of odd bacteria
that use, not oxygen, but sulfur
to survive. Below that, dark

and still. Meromictic,
the old man said, in his mind
a strangely tinted cloud
afloat on even stranger
darkness. The boy said,
That's cool. He was saying it
to himself about the hawk.

COAL BARGE ON THE OHIO

Everything empties
out of the emptiness.
Everything empty
overflows. Dawn light:
snowflakes settling
into the river,
others drifting
over the coal.

BLAST AT THE ATTIC WINDOW

The mind
at the top
of the attic stair
wheeled
in the galactic arms
of a snowstorm lit
by streetlights
from below.
Inside a spinning cloud
of stars, the mind,
in an intricate
swirl of ice,
leaned forth,
gyroscopically true,
vibrating
at the top of the stair.

HORACE, BOOK III, ODE XXVI

Girls? I lived for them,
bearing my spear in the field
with honor, now at the wall of your shrine,
o Goddess, to hang up arms

alongside harp and torch—
no more at unyielding gates
to press a young man's cause.
And yet I pray you, keeper of the island

of such pleasures, queen
of the river at Memphis where all snows melt,
give this proud girl Chloe one
exquisite flick from the tongue of your lash.

ALL CLEAR: AN INVITATION

to Dan Moriarty

The doctor took me by the genital
and jammed a camera up the tube to see,
got rosy vistas of my colon, too,
a cryptic spool unwinding on the monitor,

no anesthetic, and the pain—like flying,
banking back toward earth, my brow bone
flat against the plexiglass to watch
the vineyards and the Finger Lakes

glide west toward twilight: beauty,
Rilke says, is the beginning of a terror
we find bearable because it has disdained
serenely to destroy us. Once,

obliterated by a quart
of tepid muscatel, I lay
in piss-warm shallows with my right arm
thrust straight down a mudhole,

snatching and snatched back by
what you then a thousand miles northeast
would have assumed was bass bait
and called crabs, what supermarkets here call

crayfish. Mud bugs, I say,
and tonight I'm turning them in olive oil
with garlic, lemon juice, and thyme.
Come on over: have some.

KENNETH HAXTON, QUARTERBACK, THIRD FROM LEFT

1892–1970

His team looks deathless in their photograph,
though one would soon work horses at the front
to haul artillery, and one would do the math
to place exploding shells among the boys
our boys were facing. At Ole Miss for now,
he called the snap, and with his dancing shuffle
faded left, his friends without much padding slammed
the boys from LSU, his fingertips found
niches in the seam, and downfield the receiver
sprinted. Things kept clicking: swivel
in the hips and shoulders, forearm canting,
football risen spiraling away. "There!
That's the ticket," he said, and he took the hit.

THE INTERPRETATION OF DREAMS

Don José Vidal, a small man
with a crew of slaves, ruled
an outpost named for him Vidalia.
My great-aunts were named for him
as well. They lived nearby in a town
called Natchez, after the Notchie,
whom our tribe with muskets drove away.

My mother, Josephine, on Sunday
mornings, read to us from scripture:
Joseph came from Pharaoh's jail,
from slavery to power, by translating
truth from the outlandishness of dreams.
The seven cows in Pharaoh's dream
were seven years, he said, and he grew rich.
But seven generations later, his whole tribe
as slaves, between the walls of a divided sea,
fled Egypt, so that the walls behind them
toppled onto chariots and men with spears.

The walls of Jericho fell, too, she read.
My brothers and I shifted in our chairs,
while Joshua put man and woman, young
and old, to the sword. He killed them
all, all but the household of the harlot

with whose help the spies had done their job.
My mother said these stories were like dreams.
We try to find in them what's true.
And when we searched among the stones,
we found that Jericho fell
centuries before the birth of Joshua.

Before my birth, my mother learned
that Jesus, named for Joshua
by Joseph number two, taught John,
the student he loved most, that God
is love. It says this in the Greek
of what we call First John.
Scholars note that by the time
the author of that sermon wrote it,
John was dead. The voice, however,
with his name, still floats up
on the darkness like a dream. *Theos,*
it says, God, *ein agape,* is love.

Beside the Mississippi where we lived
old temples for the sun god burned
on earthen pyramids three centuries
before the birth of Don José Vidal.
No name, no voice, not one word
floats up on the darkness in the mounds,
only fragments of the temples burned.
My father as a boy kept goats
there, over the cotton fields
where his great-uncle, Herman
Blum, went bankrupt farming.

When I climbed there as boy, a honey
locust spine slid through my shoe sole
through my instep into the bone.
My memory of this grows vague. Years
later, archaeologists from Harvard,
excavating, found the temples,
burned on several mounds, they said,
at once. Who burned them, why,
they told me, nobody will ever know.

SHRINE

Just inside the doorframe
she sat
facing the light of sunrise,

arms held high,
her house
the one dawn

opens, hers a song
sung in the dark
mind where the flame

slips into daylight,
and her brothers
on the roof lay

peering
through the smoke hole
to observe her,

hound beside them
couchant,
listening.

SHIPWRECK: LAST THOUGHTS
OF AN ENTOMOLOGIST

Bugs flitted over the face of a ghost
that looked up out of the sea,
his own face at the stern of the lifeboat.
Sea skaters meant mangroves, islands,
water, maybe, you could drink.
If he could stand up, he would
scan for where. But now
he had to think. Bug, *bugge,*
used to mean a boogie man
or bugbear. Something vague
passed underneath his face.
He was thinking: bugs,
true bugs, included bedbugs,
water scorpions, and toe-biters.
His image in the water smiled.
In Baja, the ferocious water bug
may bite a person's toe.
A person may, for pleasure,
bite another person's toe.
The two of them in bed may coo,
or moan. Inside his face
he felt the wrench of tears,
but no tears came. Three hundred
fathoms down, in total dark,
in almost freezing calm,
a sow-bug-like crustacean, longer
than his forearm, moved its limbs.

FEBRUARY THAW

Warm wind tore the lids
off garbage cans,
and suddenly from the calm
between two banks
of endless gray
the sun's flame dazzled
snowflakes in midair.
The next gust fogged
the rattling windowpanes,
and by dark they froze.

WAIT

to Andy Robbins

Your new poem with instructions for your funeral
scared me. There's no hurry, right? Ancient scrolls
say bluebirds from the Turquoise Pond invite
the chosen to come west and pluck the peaches
of eternal life. Let's wait for that. Upstairs
across the street, where Ray sat typing his
last poems, a grade-school kid is looking out
for the eclipse. It's Christmas. Snow nonstop,
like I need this. The girls still love it,
every morning. Me, last night, I shoveled,
and before dawn, and by dusk I'll be out
shoveling again. My chances of a coronary
are dead even, and you smack funereal.
Please. When the moon had hidden half the sun,
the clouds broke, and I saw a blur that hurt.
The next eclipse on Christmas looks good
from Dakar. Let's be there, in three hundred years.

ANENT THE YELLOW FIELD, FA-LA

The blue that made the grassblades green
withdrew, and under clouds too cold for rain,
despicable, as she who loves and loathes me
says I am, I trudged the undergrowth, my song
a shame to no one in particular: fa-la: a ditty
without meaning, of no use. Where brittle, wan
with rime, the wood rush wasted underfoot,
sang I my nonsense sagely to myself: fa-la.

WHERE THINGS WERE

Venus and Mars were almost touching
in the west at nightfall. We spoke

only to the children over dinner,
not at all when they had gone to bed.

By midnight, in the torpor of my rage, I lay
beside you, thinking about our progress in the dark:

the wobbly spin of the earth, the old moon
with the sun beside it under the bedroom floor.

You snuffled while you fell asleep, then
snored, and later in a nightmare whimpered.

We kept hurtling with the sun toward Vega
somewhere past the bedroom wall, tumbling

in a spiral who knew where. I couldn't track two
movements in my mind at once, and we were spinning

seven movements deep, while in your dream
the children must have been in trouble—hurt,

I thought—your whimpers were so helpless.
I gave up my orrery, and turned and put

one arm around you, and you stirred. But we said
nothing. We just breathed, and lay awake.

COOKSTOVE

after Heraclitus

Fire kept loosening into flames
the sunlight
trees had woven into wood.

LATE WINTER, FULL MOON AT
THE END OF EUCLID

The five of us walked home from the chapel,
moonlight dusting our tongue tips when we spoke.
One of us said, In Egypt the moon belonged
to a scribe, a dog-headed ape who read
from the Book of Wisdom. This one had kissed
the mouth of the dead man. Another said,
Hundreds of miles below the craters,
almost imperceptible moonquakes tremble
in the plutonic structure. The moon
was inducting us into the grief of academics.
Leo the Tenth, our librarian said, after
he excommunicated Luther, put a moonstone
onto his tongue to let the parochial mind
dissolve into the mind of moonlight.
Stabbed by the breath of my nostrils, feeling
the ball of my foot at the curbstone, my heart
the cardiologist tells me is failing,
I looked from face to face at my friends.
When the walk light came on I said, Let's walk
into the moon at the end of Euclid, conversing
the way we did with him. Let's remember, the way
he did, the comets fallen into the southernmost craters,
the ones they say sunlight never touches.

LIBBA'S PICTURE

The way she worked you'd think
that watercolors warded off DTs.
"Two Fuzzy Birds and a Red Tree,"
she called this—big purple blurs
with blurred green eyes, tree tiny,
bright orange, green, and yellow leaves,
each color clustered on a separate branch.
It was a souvenir of detox, almost festive,
like that smile she gave me from her bed
the day she painted this, when I was five.

PROSPECTUS: IN LIEU OF THE MALL EXPANSION

to the Syracuse mayor, the county executive,
and members of Common Council

I propose a shrimp ramp,
so that the shrimp can fly
from my yard over the lilacs
into the tamarack next door,
the way infected crows
and chickadees do now.
Your scheme to make our mall
the biggest mall on earth
is boring. We could build
a shrimp ramp cheap. It's true,
there may not be an ocean here
where shrimp could live,
but river shrimpers
in my hometown sold
fine shrimp, though they
were toxic, and pollution
killed them. It was sad,
but let's not maunder.
No ramp on our scale needs
measly river shrimp.
Forget them! Let's import
Malaysian prawns:
they're bigger. What we need

is vision! Once the shrimp ramp
rears, magnificent!
against the darkness
of the civic mind, details,
like feasibility, will sort themselves.

CONSORT AT BAY WINDOW

Pine ribs in the body of a lute
glowed through with sunlight,
and a girl's breath sang
inside a hollow throat
of pearwood. Rust was smoldering
through the crowns of oaks,
while willow leaves unfastened
in the cold looked golden
as their first buds had
in spring. Through the clouds
came sounds of geese. I stopped
to listen and smelled snow.

GIMME A VISKEY

Inhaling, head tipped back, aware
that soon the world would hear him
speak, he paused, as if to sip
from an eternal English cigarette,
like Garbo on the very cusp of speech,
except nobody cared what he would say.

CONSCIOUSNESS: AN ALLEGORY

The wolf spider lies paralyzed, and no one knows
    how conscious in his higher brain,
  because a blue-black spider wasp has stung
    the lower ganglion that works his legs.

The wasp positions him, and turns to check
  her burrow before hauling him inside,
    so that her young, when hatched,
  can feed on him alive, less vital
    organs first, to keep him fresh.

Now, should a scientist just slightly
  shift this spider out of place,
    the wasp when she returns
      will reposition him
  and check the burrow yet again;

and if the scientist again disturbs the prey,
  which may for all we know still be alert,
the sequence of behaviors will repeat—again,
    and yet again, the wasp oblivious,
      it seems, till chemicals released
    inside the brain by hunger, or fatigue,
  or "recognition" trigger what they call
an understanding in the so-called scientist,
    permitting him to stop.

SUNLIGHT AFTER WARM RAIN

Brow damped by the noonday,
drops at the edge of his jaw
in coruscations, he stood still
in the shade of that same oak
he had climbed in another life
for mistletoe his mother used
to liven their front door at solstice,
that same oak where his father
now lay under the drip line.

RODAN & RAMBO VS. RIMBAUD & RODIN

to Kenneth Koch (1925–2002)

After Rimbaud wrings the neck of eloquence,
his namesake Rambo cannot speak—confused,
misunderstood, he means no harm, but has to kill
a small-town deputy, maim fifty men,
and set the town on fire to clarify.

Most audiences find Stallone as Rambo
more appealing than Rimbaud himself,
particularly when we see the poet wreck
his *bon ami* Verlaine's whole life—
Verlaine, indifferent to his children
and his wife, deranged, degraded, brings
a pistol to his mother's house
and in the bedroom wounds his incubus,
Rimbaud, who calls the cops
and has him thrown for two years
into jail in Belgium.

Rambo does time, too, for murder. Even Rimbaud
does a day, I think, for his incompetence
at stiffing a conductor for the fare.

At twenty-one, his fling with poetry and poets
flung, Rimbaud leaves home for tropical adventure
as a grunt—like Rambo, dabbling later
in the gore and filth of mercenary chic.

First names add to the confusion. Jean,
the prodigy of petulance, is Rimbaud;
John, the posterboy of peeve, is Rambo.

Rodan (the supersonic, pyropneustic,
mutated pteranodon in monster movies
from Japan) is not much like Rodin
(whose Thinker looks to me more pumped
than pensive), but raw power seems
to govern most activities of both.

Rimbaud meets Rambo in Rodin,
prodigious thirst for novelty in bed
exacerbated by a not-so-bright-boy's
passion for the ripped physique.
Rodan, more Rambolike than Rodinesque,
sets fires and runs amok. Not one man
of the three, much less the reptile,
earns renown for tenderness.

Three swift conclusions here
might be: (1) populism—cheering
for the paramilitary dash of both
Rodan and Rambo, with contempt
for the pretensions of Rimbaud and Rodin;
(2) elitism—deeming Rodin and Rimbaud
superior, or Rambo and Rodan superior,
because of psychosocial
and politico-esthetic rationales;
or (3) crypto-nihilism—disingenuous
nostalgia for the act of finding
value ever anywhere at all.

My values are *rimbaldiennes,* at least
in that his poems seem to me, in my "maturity,"
as once to him in his, beside the point,
also in my finding Rambo fun to watch.

Rodin I loved when I was seventeen
and wanted muscles more like those
he sculpted, to attract girls more
like those he sculpted and seduced,
which still seems theoretically
worthwhile, although the aftertaste
of Rodin's oeuvre on my palate now
is schmaltzier than it is fiery.

For true fieriness of palate, Rodan rules.
He's bigger, meaner, faster, and more
charismatic than the other three,
and better looking than Godzilla, too,
the roundedness about whose muzzle
always struck me as a little mawkish.

We bohemians, however, most of us,
prefer the goddess Mothra, the benevolent
Rodan-sized moth with fairies
in kimonos singing on board in their cage.
She guards an island paradise
of high symbolic consummation,
wherefore every mortal yearns,
though my preadolescent wonder
at the strangeness up there on the screen
has dwindled. What I need
to see me through late middle age

may be that female touch
of tremulous, huge, feathery antennae.

Meanwhile, on Baudelaire and Bogart,
on *beaux idéals* in general,
I will be forever unironic
in my praise, but not today.

MOTHS

Lacking a mouth,
the luna moth
may thirst
but cannot drink,
its body built
only to mate.

Underwings
fret endlessly
at the electric light.
Collectors say
they also flock
to sugar water
on a birch trunk.

Females of the species
we call psyche (soul),
or the bagworm moth,
lack wings and legs.
They sometimes kill
the ornamental evergreens
in which they nest.

The sphinx, amazingly,
drinks honey
from inside the hive,

and nectar
from the blossom
of the bittersweet
(or nightshade).

Melancholy souls
should not abuse
the nightshade,
which one expert calls
the grape from hell.
Joy's grape is better,
he maintains,
for brains like his,
that turn
under the full noontide
insanely sad.

UNTITLED

from the German of Paul Celan

Inside them was earth,
and they dug.

They dug and they dug, while day passed
and night. They did not praise God,
who, they heard, wanted things so,
who, they heard, knew things were so.

They dug and they heard nothing more.
They did not grow wise, they made no new song,
they contrived not one word to speak.
They dug.

A calm came over them, also a storm,
and the seas came all on all.
I dig, you dig, the worm digs as well,
and the singing in air says: they dig.

O one, o none, o no one, o you:
Where has the going nowhere gone?
I dig and you dig and I dig toward you—
and here at the finger awakens the ring.

STORM

Cattle egrets in the dry grass waded
like white clerics at the hooves
of brood cows, heifers, and new calves.

Forked lightning. Calm.
The darkness in the cattle tank welled up
and flooded the reflection of the trees.

Turkey vultures wheeled, and wheeled away.
No swifts, no swallows, children gone indoors.
Rain seethed into the willowtops,

sky flashing, while the black bull
under the water locust glowed
with an inward surge of darkness.

IF I MAY

on receiving an award for poetry

I would like to thank (besides my family, you,
my teachers, friends, and readers) hydrogen
for fueling the stars without which poetry
would not exist. The sun has been *the* star
most crucial to my work, but distant stars
have been there for me, too, and planets, meteors,
the moon. About the moon, I'm grateful
that our boys left flags up there, and brought back
rocks and dust. I'd like to thank the dust.
The oceans may or may not have put
molecules together that first time
to form a living cell, but I would like
to thank the oceans for that dreamy look
they give us when the cameras turn toward Earth
from outer space. My thankfulness today
toward what they call "the emptiness of space"
is inexpressible. But empty? Space, for me,
is full of intersecting waves of light
and curved dimensionalities of being infinitely
numerous yet one. God I want to thank
especially, if He exists, which I believe
He does. He may not. Probably not.
But I would like to thank Him. Thanks.

SCREECH-OWL PIE

to Roger Fanning in memory of Tom Andrews
and Agha Shahid Ali

A mouse, let's say white-footed,
spooked by headlights, dashed
from under the shoulder grass, owl
stooped, and here beside the road:

owl pie—a body sacred once
to worshippers of wisdom and dark fate,
now mashed into a feathered plaque
with only wings and talons left intact.

My brain beside the road,
unlike the owl brain eaten by a crow,
felt sun burst into the forward ports,
intense as headlights bearing down . . .

to think: the mouse the car set free
might well have been the species
people train to sing
for ears of wheat. And friends of ours

who taught with us by that same road,
though dead, may train us yet
to sing for them, to say, by reading
from their poems, how beautiful

Kashmir and West Virginia are
without them. Screech-owl pie, wings
spread with talons underneath, contains
no more an owl than shut books do

friends. And as for us who happen by,
who hunker at the guardrail: listen.
Year-round after nightfall
the white-footed mice are singing.

PRATT'S FALLS, NY

The creek drops more than a hundred feet,
fanned out across the rocks. It trickles
down through gravel into pools on shelves
where vetch and knotweed flower
out of the cracks. Not much flow this time
of year, but you should see how red the sumac
is for August. Mastodons grazed here,
until a glacier snatched the hillside
out from under the little creek, which now
has had to do a pratfall off the cliff
for what, ten thousand years? Manoah Pratt
did own it, if a man can own a watergod.
He died, in any case, about the time
McCormick patented the reaper.

AFTER, AFTER, AND BEYOND

After the cobweb frost on roses,
after the dawn snow hidden
under a thicker snow by dusk,
beyond the noon thaw and the freeze
at midnight, when the old magnolias
finally bloomed with freckles of decay
already burning through their rouge
and white, I knelt among the petals
fallen in the first spring heat,
and smelled violets and dirt and grass.

BREATHLESS

to Dr. Robert Harris McCarter, psychologist

With psyche baffled by the common cold,
and sinuses pulsating, I read books
about the problems in my head, and drink.

Vesalius, who sawed the tops off skulls
to map the secret chambers in the brain,
was sentenced by the Church to burn alive,
for noting that the brain and not the heart
housed consciousness. They would have let him make
a pilgrimage instead, except he died
en route of fever.

           True anatomy,
they said, came from the Greek of Galen.
In his book, the hypothalamus,
left feverish by *phlegma* (flame), made phlegm,
which drained and cooled the *psyche* (meaning breath).
Green nose goop (that's *pituita* in Latin,
here patooie) was gray matter. Brains,
in other words, leaked out your nose from what
my source describes as a "small somewhat
cherry-shaped double structure attached
by a stalk to the base of the midbrain,"
your so-called pituitary.

About the common cold,
Descartes, who died of one, and all the doctors
since antiquity were wrong. But when they thought
pituitaries must affect the humors
we call hormones they were right! Descartes,
of course, believed the soul exhorts the flesh
at just one spot, in the pineal gland.
Behind the nose, the known world is a bubble
trembling in a cup of bone.

                The nose itself,
if everything were turned to smoke, would be
the seat of judgment, Heraclitus said.
He thought, in the abysmal dark, the soul
is known by scent.

           If I could breathe,
it might inspire my soul, but Æolus,
the god who stirs the breath of wind, the soul
of soul, has left me breathless.

            Whiskey helps,
they say, though Coleridge, drunk at thirty, dulled
with pain, his marriage failing, opium
unmanning him, heard Æolus, the world
soul, sob and moan and, when the storm hit, scream
in his æolian lute, and nothing helped.

Under the midbrain, over the pharynx,
in a tiny hollow in the lower skull,
a cherry dangles from the infundibulum
and synthesizes humors that induce

the glands to tell the cells to grow,
and yearn, and rage—and reproduce.

This fire attended by the soul, this *phlegma*
in the center of the head, is also called
in Greek *hypophysis*, or undergrowth. The soul
is crouching in the undergrowth. Tears form,
I snuffle, things look blurred, but I can feel,
as Heraclitus felt, in *pyr aéizöon* my soul,
a breath inside an everliving flame.

WHEREABOUTS UNKNOWN

Lost under the missile fire and bombs,
this small man carved in stone,
bare-chested in a skirt of tufted wool,
hands folded at the sternum, pleads
with him who takes us in his net:
the tall god vast as earth, his beard
in ropes of braid, wings spread, arising
like the lion-headed eagle flanked by stags.

BONFIRE

Wellfleet, 2006

Wind from the ocean
swept smoke into the hair
and into the faces of boys
and old men, women and schoolgirls,
some of us laughing, some of us
staring into the flames. One played guitar,
and others sang, some talked,
some looked up into the stars,
and under the dark face of the dune
waves broke with an audible hush.
One high-school boy was pointing out
a speck of nighttime sunlight
on the hull of a space station
two hundred miles away, a suite
of rooms, with astronauts inside
just floating, weightless. His great-uncle
lay with his head on a pillow of sand.
Fifty years ago, the old man said,
our neighbors' house stood there.
He was pointing into the sky, midair,
into a cloud of ash, his right hand
trembling, That's where the lip
of the dune was then. He laughed:
My girlfriend lived there. After the speck
in the stars blinked out, the boy said,
That, for them, was a sunset.

And the Milky Way hung in the smoke
over the breaking waves
where the kitchen had stood
when the neighbor girl at the table
blushed and squeezed his hand.

BLUE MOUNTAIN

Pierced to the deep rock
with noon sunlight,
Fisher Pond
by nightfall lies
under a starless sky
opaque. At their fire
the lovers want
what might be theirs,
if only . . . *Who,*
the hoot owl calls,
and later, *You,*
he seems to say,
You, and the fog drifts
into the campfire.

SONG OF THE INDIGO BUNTING

"Fire fire! Where where? Here here."

Blue: three down-curved
dark-blue yellow-throated
sepals and three upright
narrower blue petals, swamp flag,
flame shape from the grave
beside the river. Listen:

indigo bunting, blue
with black wings soon to carry him
all night on the gulf wind to the island.
"Fire fire!" he keeps singing, song
learned in another world: "Where where?"
And if he cannot see the stars he sickens.

Depth of a bell rung after sunset.
Blue, in the eye where joy veers
into sadness, veers, and deepens.
Red tide in the surf at midnight,
blue with luminescence, ocean
turning over in the mind a question.

And in the master's palm the yellow
of an egg, still perfect, to be spilled
into the powder of crushed lapis
put to heaven with small brushstrokes:

blue, beyond the schizophreniform
wild hairdo of the Baptist. Where?

Where in death is the soul? Dawn,
where the Seven Sisters swim
and vanish. Hind wing of a swallowtail.
Subterranean blue crystal tears of copper.
Here, among small yellow blossoms
in the sour grass, blue flutes of gentian.

Where is the music lips formed
out of nothing? Planet earth,
blue-green as an opal. Here. Here
at my feet at the path's edge, berries
of a bluebeard lily, blue as sapphires,
blue with frost and poison.

GIFT

All our righteousnesses are as filthy rags;
and we all do fade as a leaf

—Isaiah 64:6

After my mother's father died,
she gave me his morocco Bible.
I took it from her hand, and saw
the gold was worn away, the binding
scuffed and ragged, split below the spine,
and inside, smudges where her father's
right hand gripped the bottom corner
page by page, an old man waiting, not quite
reading the words he had known by heart
for sixty years: our parents in the garden,
naked, free from shame; the bitterness of labor;
blood in the ground, still calling for God's
curse—his thumbprints fading after the flood,
to darken again where God bids Moses smite
the rock, and then again in Psalms, in Matthew
every page. And where Paul speaks of things
God hath prepared, things promised them who wait,
things not yet entered into the loving heart,
below the margin of the verse, the paper
is translucent with the oil and dark
still with the dirt of his right hand.

Acknowledgments

The author thanks the editors of the following publications where poems in this collection first appeared, some of them under different titles and in different form.

The Atlantic Monthly: "Gift," "Datura," "The Invention of a Written Word for God in Sumer"

Triquarterly: "Shrine," "Bedroom Window Crusted Thick with Ice," "Anent the Yellow Field, Fa-la," "Whereabouts Unknown"

Cortland Review: "Bert, in Memory, and Herb Robert," "If I May," "All Clear: An Invitation," "Wait"

The Hudson Review: "Letter from Syracuse"

The Kenyon Review: "Song of the Indigo Bunting"

Oxford American: "Kenneth Haxton, Quarterback, Third from Right"

Panhandler: "Breathless," "Rodan & Rambo vs. Rimbaud & Rodin"

Shenandoah: "Consciousness: An Allegory," "The Cry of the Snowy Tree Cricket"

Smartish Place: "After, After, and Beyond," "Consort at Bay Window"

Stone Canoe: "Isaac's Room, Empty, 4 A.M.," "Blast at the Attic Window," "Shipwreck: Last Thoughts of an Entomologist," "Cookstove"

Verbal Seduction: "Horace, Book III, Ode XXVI"

Thanks also to friends and family, and to Deborah Garrison, whose gifts as a poet and editor have made her help with my work invaluable.

A Note on the Type

The text of this book was set in a typeface called Aldus, designed by the celebrated typographer Hermann Zapf in 1952–1953. Based on the classical proportion of the popular Palatino type family, Aldus was originally adapted for Linotype composition as a slightly lighter version that would read better in smaller sizes. Hermann Zapf was born in Nuremberg, Germany, in 1918. He has created many other well known typefaces including Comenius, Hunt Roman, Marconi, Melior, Michelangelo, Optima, Saphir, Sistina, Zapf Book and Zapf Chancery.

Composed by Stratford Publishing Services,
Brattleboro, Vermont
Printed and bound by Thomson-Shore,
Dexter, Michigan
Designed by Anthea Lingeman